M000122196

Cover photo: Jen Rosenstein

Ukulele by Chris Kringel

ISBN 978-1-4803-6706-7

7777 W. BLUEMOUND RD. P.O. BOX 13819 MILWAUKEE, WI 53213

In Australia Contact:
Hal Leonard Australia Pty. Ltd.
4 Lentara Court
Cheltenham, Victoria, 3192 Australia
Email: ausadmin@halleonard.com.au

Visit Hal Leonard Online at
www.halleonard.com

UKULELE NOTATION LEGEND

THE MUSICAL STAFF shows pitches and rhythms and is divided by bar lines into measures. Pitches are named after the first seven letters of the alphabet.

TABLATURE graphically represents the ukulele fingerboard. Each horizontal line represents a a string, and each number represents a fret.

Notes:

Strings:

2nd string, 3rd fret   1st & 2nd strings open, played together   open F chord

HALF-STEP BEND: Strike the note and bend up 1/2 step.

WHOLE-STEP BEND: Strike the note and bend up one step.

GRACE NOTE BEND: Strike the note and immediately bend up as indicated.

SLIGHT (MICROTONE) BEND: Strike the note and bend up 1/4 step.

BEND AND RELEASE: Strike the note and bend up as indicated, then release back to the original note. Only the first note is struck.

PRE-BEND: Bend the note as indicated, then strike it.

VIBRATO: The string is vibrated by rapidly bending and releasing the note with the fretting hand.

HAMMER-ON: Strike the first (lower) note with one finger, then sound the higher note (on the same string) with another finger by fretting it without picking.

PULL-OFF: Place both fingers on the notes to be sounded. Strike the first note and without picking, pull the finger off to sound the second (lower) note.

LEGATO SLIDE: Strike the first note and then slide the same fret-hand finger up or down to the second note. The second note is not struck.

SHIFT SLIDE: Same as legato slide, except the second note is struck.

TRILL: Very rapidly alternate between the notes indicated by continuously hammering on and pulling off.

TREMOLO PICKING: The note is picked as rapidly and continuously as possible.

NOTE: Tablature numbers in parentheses mean:

1. The note is being sustained over a system (note in standard notation is tied), or

2. The note is sustained, but a new articulation (such as a hammer-on, pull-off, slide or vibrato) begins, or

3. The note is a barely audible "ghost" note (note in standard notation is also in parentheses).

Additional Musical Definitions

 (accent)
- Accentuate note (play it louder)

(staccato)
- Play the note short

D.S. al Coda
- Go back to the sign (𝄋), then play until the measure marked "***To Coda***," then skip to the section labelled "**Coda**."

D.C. al Fine
- Go back to the beginning of the song and play until the measure marked "***Fine***" (end).

N.C.
- No chord.

- Repeat measures between signs.

- When a repeated section has different endings, play the first ending only the first time and the second ending only the second time.

CONTENTS

Butterfly

Words and Music by Jason Mraz

First note

Intro
Moderately ♩ = 108

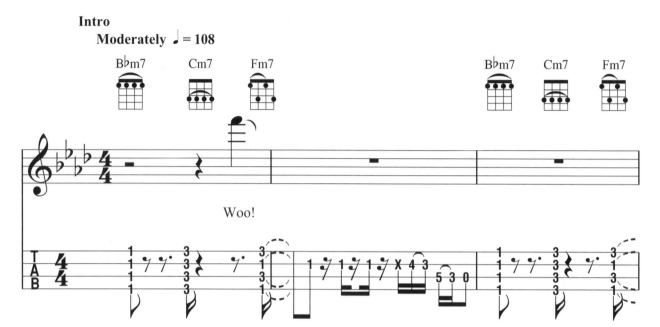

Woo!

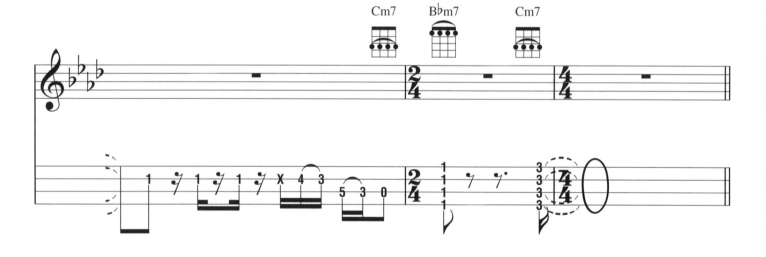

Verse

1. I'm tak-ing a mo - ment, just __ i - mag - in - ing __ that I'm danc - ing __ with

Bbm7

you. _____ I'm your pole and all you're wear - ing is ___ your

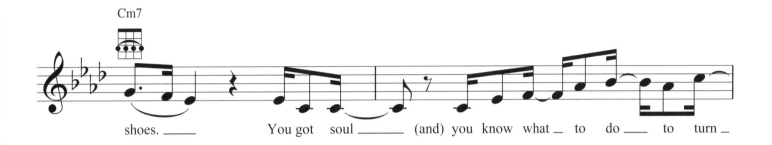

Cm7

shoes. _____ You got soul _____ (and) you know what ___ to do ___ to turn ___

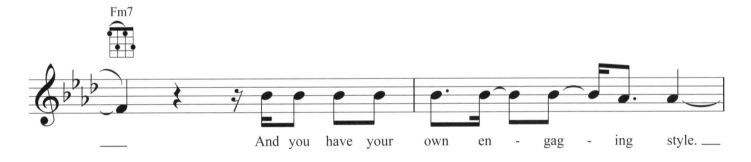

Dbmaj7   C7

___ me on ___ un - til I write ___ a song ___ a - bout ___ you. _____

Fm7

___ And you have your own en - gag - ing style. ___

Bbm7

___ And you've got the knack to ___ viv - i - fy. ___

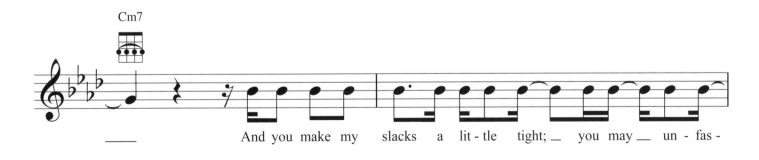

Cm7

____ And you make my slacks a lit - tle tight; ___ you may ___ un - fas -

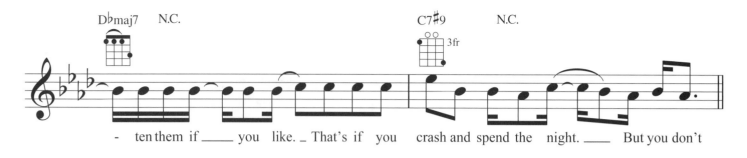

- ten them if ___ you like. ___ That's if you crash and spend the night. ___ But you don't

% Chorus

fold (and) you don't fade. ___ You got ev - 'ry - thing ___ you need, ___ es - pe - cial - ly me. ___

___ Sis - ter, you've got it all. ___ You make the call ___

To Coda ⊕

___ to make ___ my day. ___ (And) in ___ your mes - sage say ___ my name. ___ Your talk is

all the talk. ___ Sis - ter, you've got it all. _____

You've got it all. ___

2. Curl __ your up-per lip _____ up and let me look a-round.

Ride __ your tongue a-long __ your bot - tom lip, __ then bite __ down. __

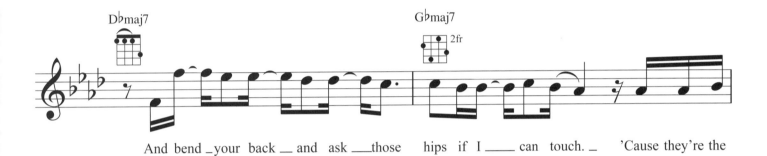

And bend __ your back __ and ask __ those hips if I ___ can touch. __ 'Cause they're the

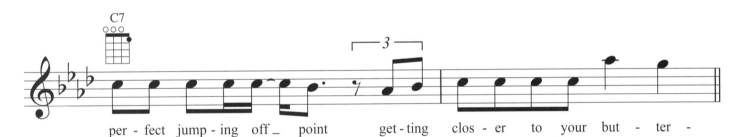

per - fect jump-ing off __ point get-ting clos - er to your but - ter -

Pre-Chorus

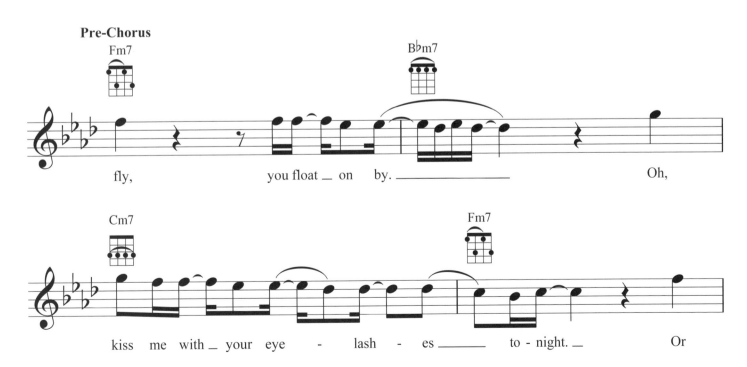

fly, you float __ on by. _____ Oh,

kiss me with __ your eye - lash - es _____ to - night. __ Or

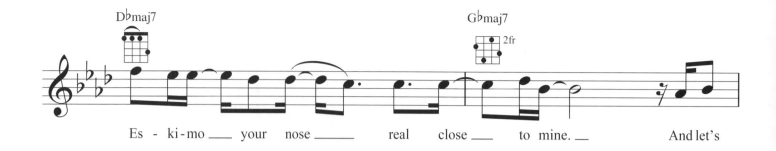

Es - ki-mo ___ your nose _____ real close ___ to mine. ___ And let's

D.S. al Coda

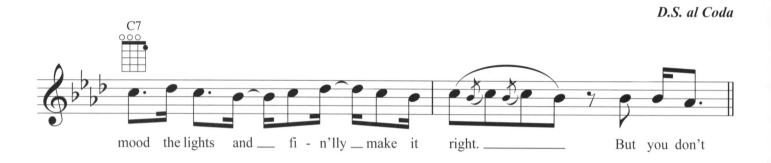

mood the lights and ___ fi - n'lly ___ make it right. _____ But you don't

Coda

all the talk. ___ Sis - ter, you've got it all. _____ You've got ___ it all, ___

___ you've got ___ it all, ___ you've got ___ it all. _____ You've got ___ it all, ___

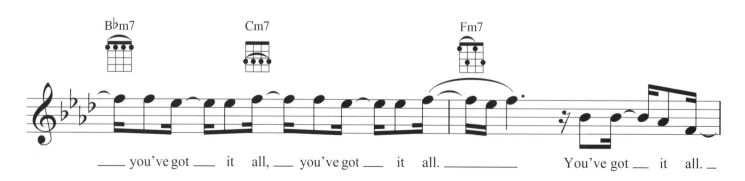

___ you've got ___ it all, ___ you've got ___ it all. _____ You've got ___ it all. ___

You've got it a-

- a - all. ___

Bridge

Doll, I need to see you pull your knee socks up (and)

let me feel you up - side down, slide in - side out, slide

o - ver here. ___ Climb ___ in - to my mouth ___ now, ___ child.

Interlude

Scat...

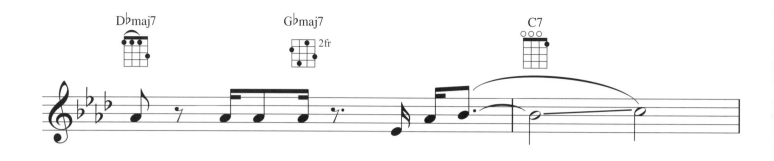

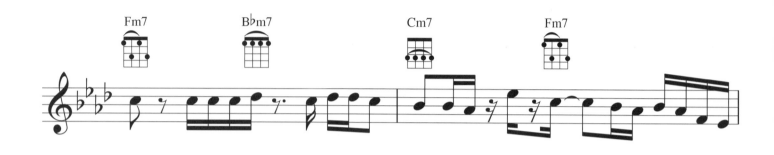

But - ter -

Pre-Chorus

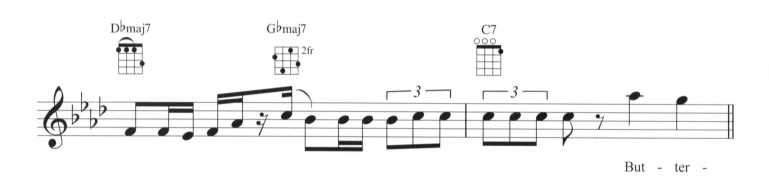

fly,   well, you land - ed on _____ my mind. ___   Damn right you

land - ed on ___ my ear ___ and then ___ you crawled ___ in - side. ___   And now ___

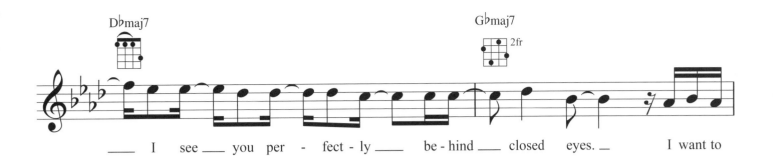

I see you per - fect - ly be - hind closed eyes. I want to

fly with you. And I don't want to lie to you. 'Cause I, 'cause I can't re - call

Chorus

a bet - ter day, sun com - ing to shine on the oc - ca - sion. You're an o -

- pen - mind - ed la - dy; you've got it all. And I nev - er

for - get a face 'cept for may - be my own. I have my days. Let's face the fact

_____ here, it's you _____ who's got it all. _____ You know _ that for-

- tune fa - vors the brave. Well, let me get paid while I make you break - fast. The rest _

_____ is up _ to you. You make the call. _____ You make the call _

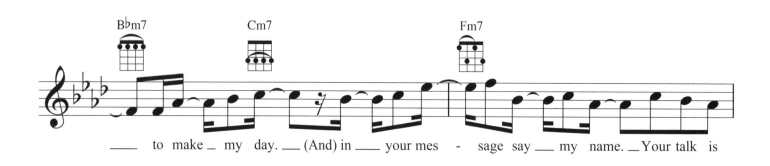

_____ to make _ my day. _ (And) in _____ your mes - sage say _ my name. _ Your talk is

all the talk. _ Sis - ter, you've got it all. _____ I can't re - call _

Hey! __ You've got __ it all.

__ you've got __ it all, __ you've got __ it all.) __

__ Woo! __ You've got, you, __ you've got it all. __

__ Hey! __ You gots, you gots, you gots, you got __ it all. __

__ Oh! __ You've got, you've got it all. __ Hey! __

But - ter - fly, __

ba - by, __ well, you got it all. __

14

I Won't Give Up

Words and Music by Jason Mraz and Michael Natter

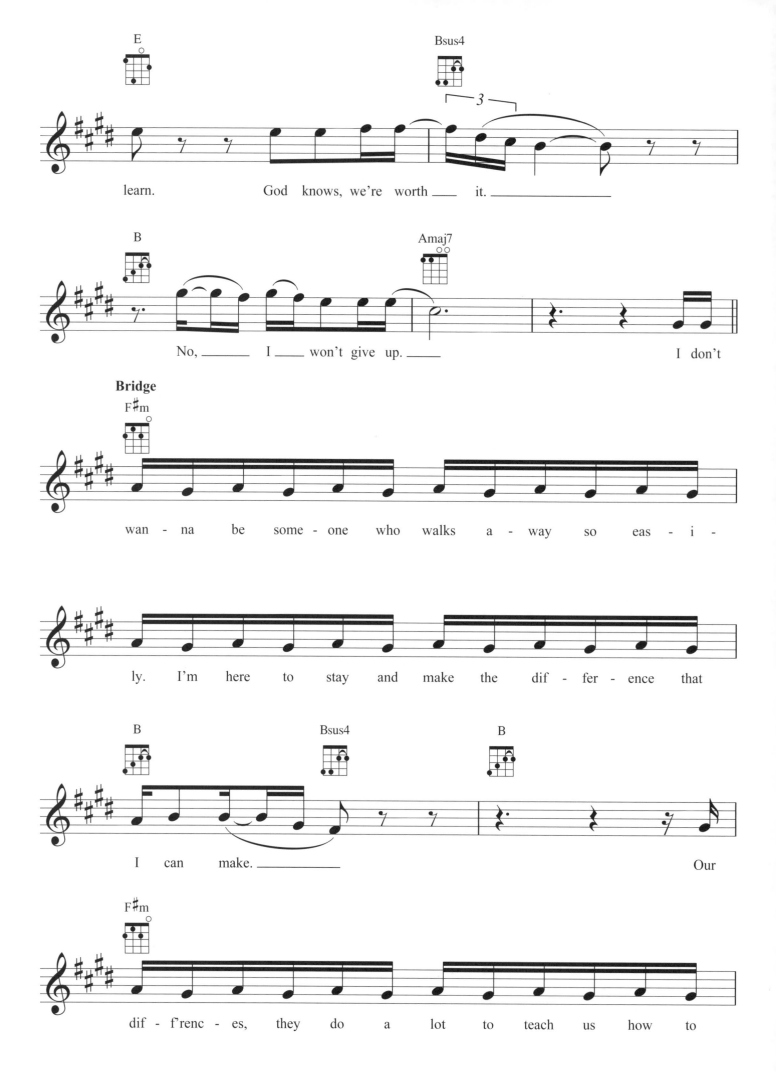

use the tools and gifts we got; yeah, we got a lot ___

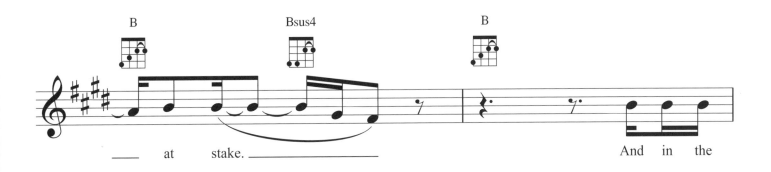

___ at stake. ___ And in the

end, you're still my friend; at least we did in - tend for

us to work. We did - n't break; we did - n't burn.

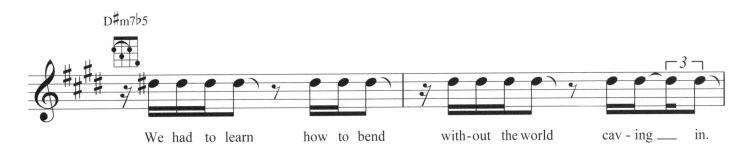

We had to learn how to bend with-out the world cav - ing ___ in.

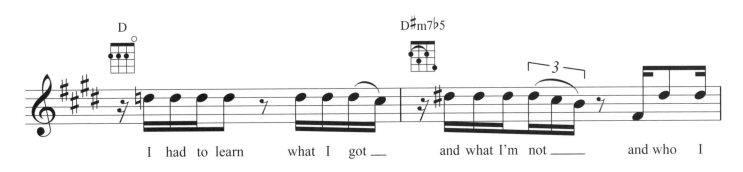

I had to learn what I got ___ and what I'm not ___ and who I

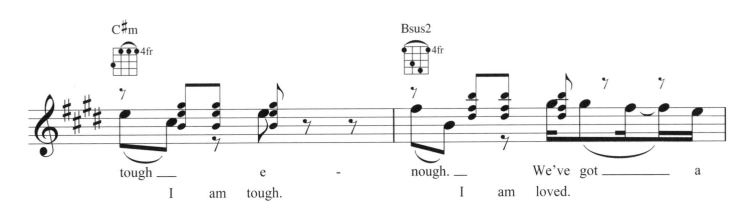

tough _____ e - nough. _____ We've got _____ a
I am tough. I am loved.

lot _____ to learn. God knows, we're worth __
We're a - live; we are loved.

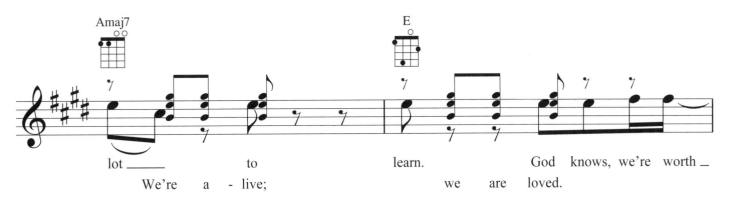

___ it. _____
And we're worth ___ it.) _____
I won't give

Outro-Chorus

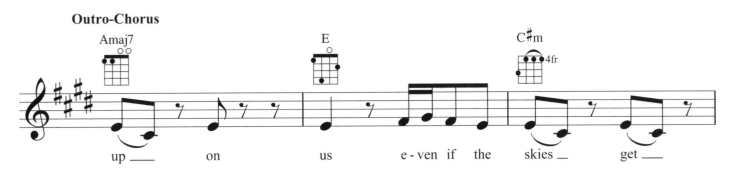

up ___ on us e-ven if the skies ___ get ___

rough. _ I'm giv-ing _ you all _____ my love. I'm still look-ing up. _____

TRACK 5

I'm Yours
Words and Music by Jason Mraz

First note

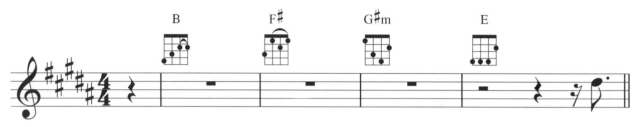

1. Well,

you done done ___ me in; you bet I felt ___ it. I
way too long ___ check - ing my tongue in the mir - ror and

tried to be chill, ___ but you're so hot that I melt - ed. I
bend - ing o - ver back - wards just to try to see it clear - er. But

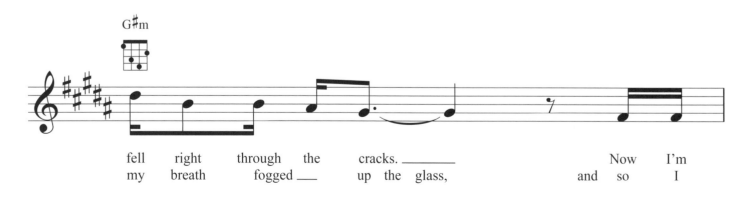

fell right through the cracks. _____ Now I'm
my breath fogged ___ up the glass, and so I

E

try - ing   to   get ____   back. _____   Be - fore   the
drew   a   new   face ____   and I laughed. _____   I

B

cool   done   run   out,   I'll   be   giv - ing   it   my   best - est,   and
guess   what   I'll   be   say - ing   is   there   ain't   no   bet - ter   rea - son   to

F♯

noth - ing's   gon - na   stop   me   but   di - vine   in - ter - ven - tion.   I
rid   your - self   of   van - i - ties   and   just   go   with   the   sea - sons.   It's

G♯m

reck - on   it's   a - gain   my   turn ____   to
what   we   aim   to   do.   Our ____

To Coda ⊕

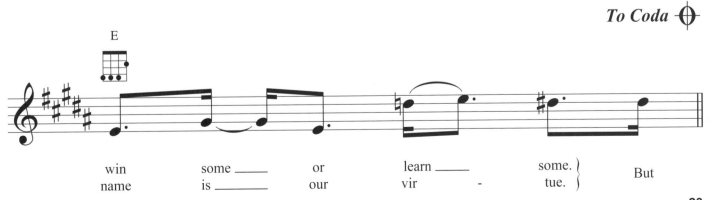

E

win   some ____   or   learn ____   some.)
name   is ____   our   vir - tue.)   But

Chorus

I ___ won't hes - i - tate no more, ___ no _____

more. ___ It can - not wait. I'm yours. _____

Verse

2. Well, o - pen up your mind and see ___ like me. ___

___ O - pen up your plans and damn, ___ you're free.

Look in - to your heart ___ and you'll ___ find love, love, ___ love, love.

24

Interlude

need ___ to com-pli - cate. Our ___ time ___ is _____ short. ___ This is our fate. I'm yours. _____ *Scat sing...*

Skooch on o - ver clos - er, dear, and I will nib - ble your ear. ___

_____ *Scat sing...*

D.S. al Coda

3. I've been spend - ing

𝄋 **Coda**

Breakdown-Chorus

I ___ won't hes - i - tate no more, ___ no _____

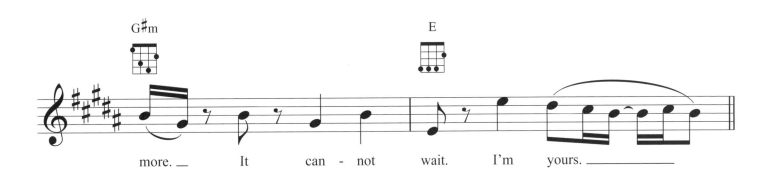

more. __ It can - not wait. I'm yours. _____

Chorus

O - pen up your mind and see like me. __

(I won't hes - i -

O - pen up your plans and, damn, __ you're __ free. __

tate no more, no

Look in - to your heart __ and you'll __ find __ that

more. It can - not

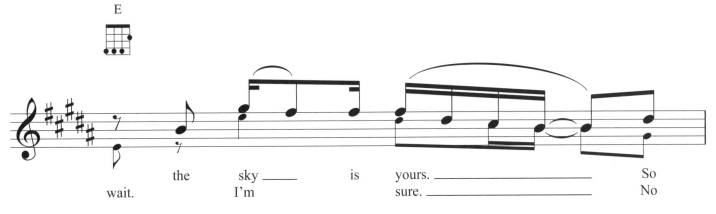

the sky ___ is yours. _____ So

wait. I'm sure. _____ No

The Remedy
(I Won't Worry)

Words and Music by Graham Edwards, Scott Spock,
Lauren Christy and Jason Mraz

First note

Intro
Moderately ♩ = 95

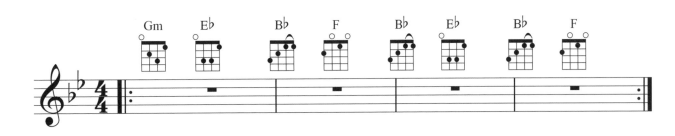

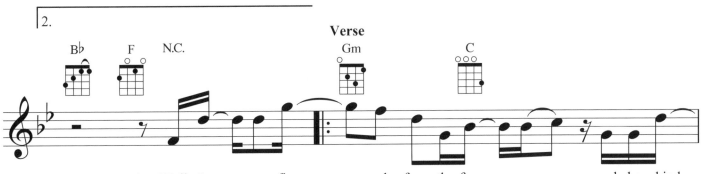

1. Well, I ___ saw fire - works from the free - way, ___ and be - hind ___
men talk - ing on the ra - di - o in a cross -

___ closed eyes ___ I can - not make them go a - way 'cause you were
-fire kind ___ of new re - al - i - ty show. ___ Un -

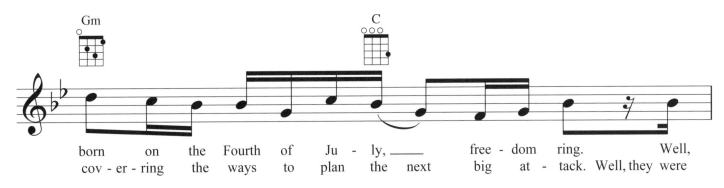

born on the Fourth of Ju - ly, ___ free - dom ring. Well,
cov - er - ring the ways to plan the next big at - tack. Well, they were

some-thing on the sur - face, it stings. I said some-
count - ing down the ways to stab the broth - er in the... be right back

- thing on the sur - face, well, it kind of makes me nerv - ous. Who says
af - ter this, the un - a - void - a - ble kiss, where the

that you de - serve this, and what kind of God would serve this? We will
min - ty fresh death breath is sure to out - last his ca -

cure this dirt - y old ___ dis - ease. Well, if
tas - tro - phe. Dance ___ with me, 'cause if

you've gots the poi - son, I've ___ gots the rem - e - dy. } The
you've gots the poi - son, I've ___ gots the rem - e - dy. }

Pre-Chorus

rem - e - dy ___ is the ex - pe - ri - ence. This is a

30

dan - ger - ous ____ li - ai - son. I ____ says, the

com - e - dy ____ is that it's se - ri - ous. This is a

strange e - nough _ new play ____ on words. __ I say, the

trag - e - dy is how you're gon - na ____ spend __ the rest __

____ of your nights _ with the light ___ on. So shine the

light on all ____ of your friends, _____ when it

all ____ a - mounts to noth - ing in ____ the end.

Chorus

I, _____ I won't wor - ry my life ____

____ a - way. ____ Hey. _____ Oh, _____ oh. ____

1.

I, _____ I won't wor - ry my life ____

____ a - way. ____ Hey. _____ Oh, _____ oh, ____

whoa.

ry when I'm mak-ing up my mind. ___ You can turn off the sun, ___

___ but I'm still gon-na shine, ___ and then I'll tell you why. ___
(Turn off the sun.) ___

Pre-Chorus

Be-cause the rem-e-dy is the ex-per-i-ence. This is a

dan-ger-ous ___ li-ai - son. I ___ says, the

com-e-dy is that it's se - ri - ous. This is a

strange e - nough ___ new play ___ on words. ___ I say, the

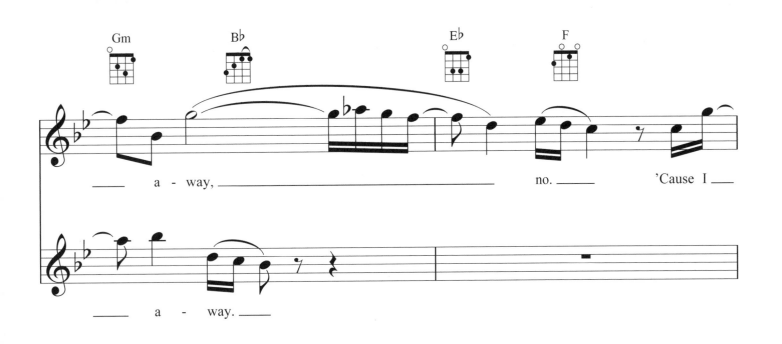

Repeat and fade

Lucky

TRACK 7

Words and Music by Jason Mraz, Colbie Caillat and Timothy Fagan

First note

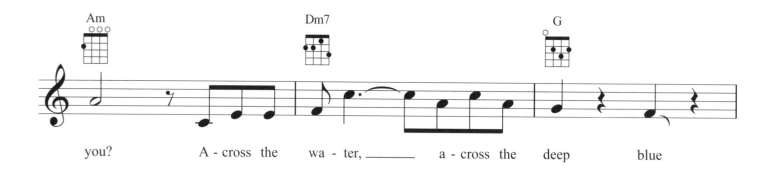

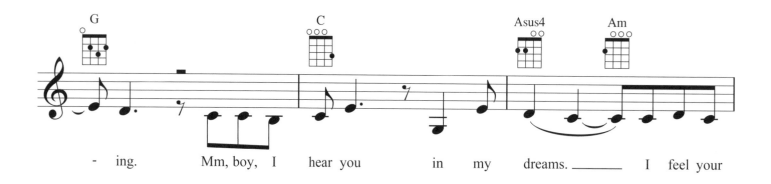

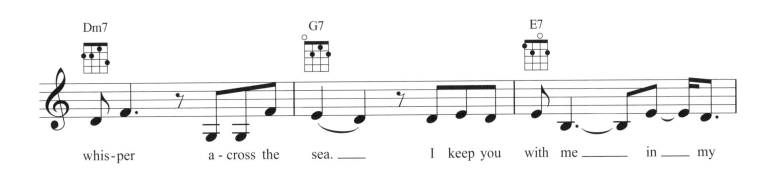

whis-per   a - cross the   sea. ___   I   keep you   with me ____ in ___ my

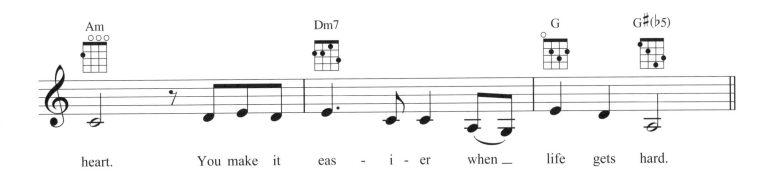

heart.   You make it   eas - i - er   when __ life   gets   hard.

Chorus
Half-time feel

Luck - y   I'm in ____ love   with my best __ friend, __   luck - y   to   have __

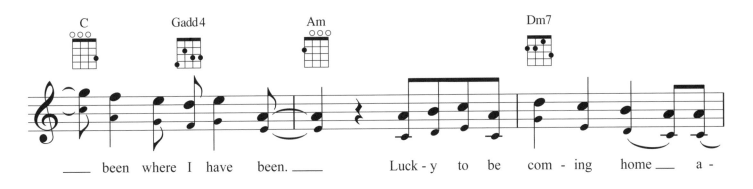

__ been where I have   been. __   Luck - y   to   be   com - ing   home __ a -

Interlude

- gain. ___   Oo, _____

𝄉 Chorus

luck - y I'm in ____ love with my best friend, ___ luck - y to have ___

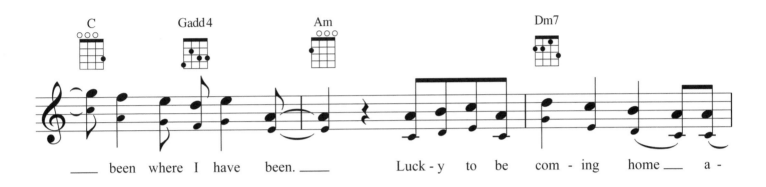

____ been where I have been. ___ Luck - y to be com - ing home ___ a -

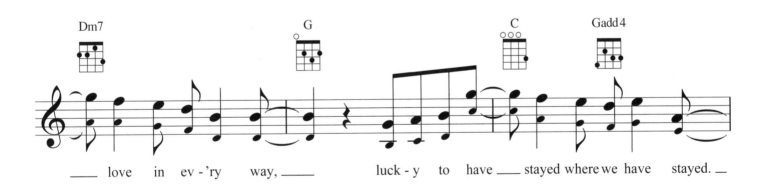

- gain. _____ Luck - y we're in ___

____ love in ev -'ry way, ___ luck - y to have ___ stayed where we have stayed. ___

To Coda ⊕

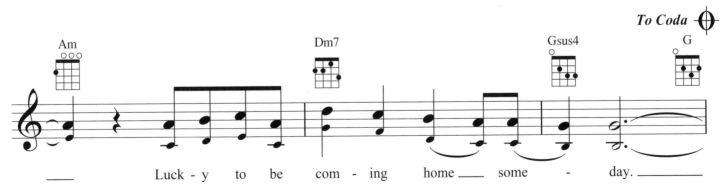

____ Luck - y to be com - ing home ___ some - day. ___

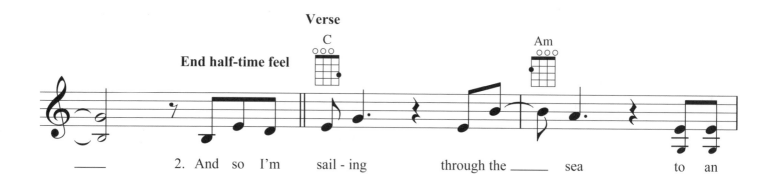

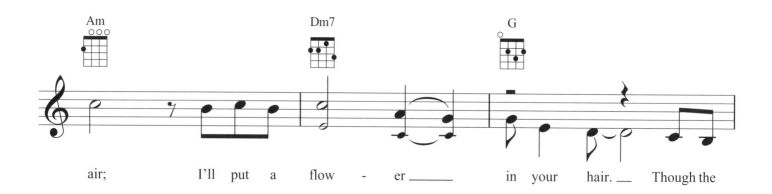

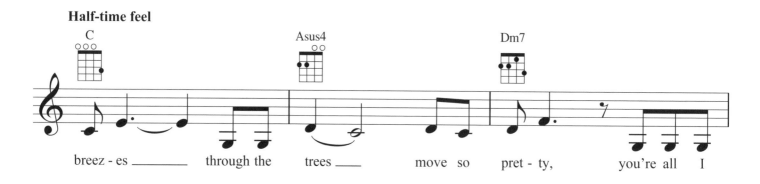

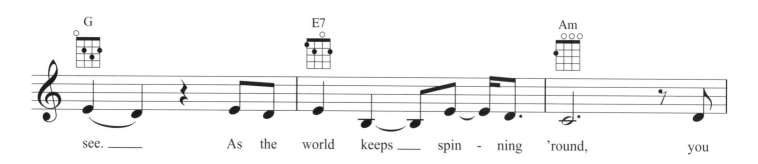

42

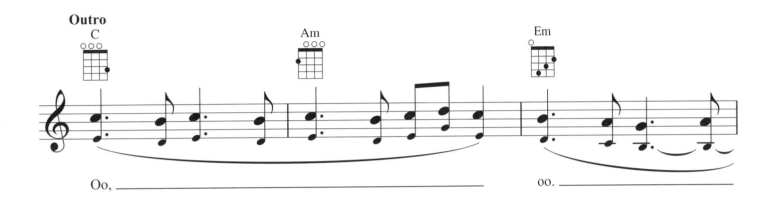

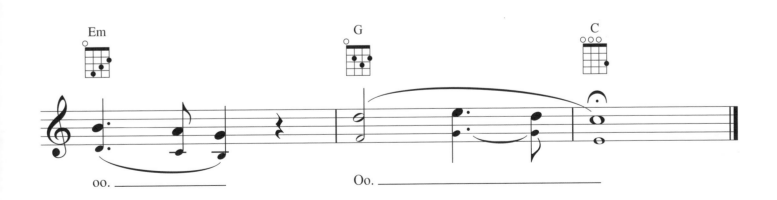

Make It Mine

Words and Music by Jason Mraz

First note

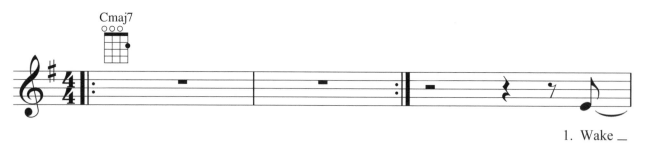

Intro
Moderately ♩ = 150

1. Wake —

Verse

—— up, ev - 'ry - one. —— How —— can you sleep —— at a time ——

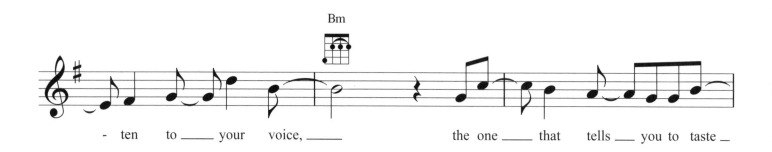

—— like   this? —— Un - less the dream - er is the real   you. —— Lis -

- ten   to —— your   voice, ——   the one —— that   tells —— you to taste ——

- ful and stead - y, _____ and rev - el - ing in en - er - gy that

ev - 'ry - one's _ e - mit - ting.   Well, I don't wan - na wait _

Outro-Chorus

_____ no more. _____   Oh, _____ I _____

_____ wan - na cel - e - brate the whole _____ world. I'm gon - na make _____ it mine. _

_____   Oh, yes, I'm _____   fol - low - ing your _

_____ joy. I'm gon - na make _____ it mine _____ be - cause I, _____

93 Million Miles

Words and Music by Jason Mraz, Michael Natter and Mike Daly

First note

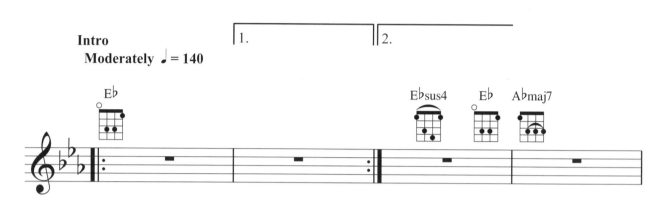

1. Nine-ty-three mil-lion miles __ from the sun. Peo-ple, get read-y, get
   hun-dred for-ty thou-sand miles __ from the moon. We've come a long way to be-long __

read-y 'cause here it comes. It's a light, a beau - ti-ful light, __ o -
__ here to share this view of the night, a glor - i-ous night. __ O -

- ver the ho - ri - zon, in - to our eyes. __ Oh, ____ my, my, __ how __
- ver the ho - ri - zon is an - oth - er bright sky. Oh, ____ my, my, __ how __

beau - ti - ful. Oh, ____ my beau - ti - ful moth- er, she told me,
beau - ti - ful. Oh, ____ my ir - re - fut - a - ble fath - er, he told me,

"Son, in __ life you're gon - na go far. __ If _____ you do it right, you'll love __
"Son, some - times it may ___ seem dark, _ but the ab-sense of the light is a

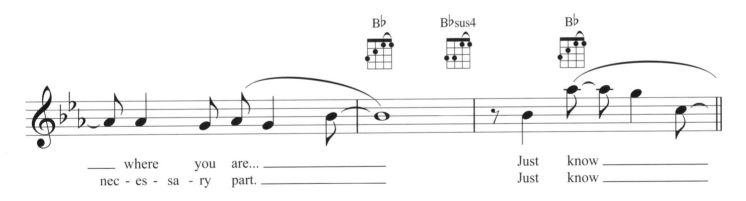

____ where you are... _____ Just know _____
nec - es - sa - ry part. _____ Just know _____

Chorus

_____ wher- ev - er you go, _____ you can al -
_____ your nev- er a - lone, _____ you can al -

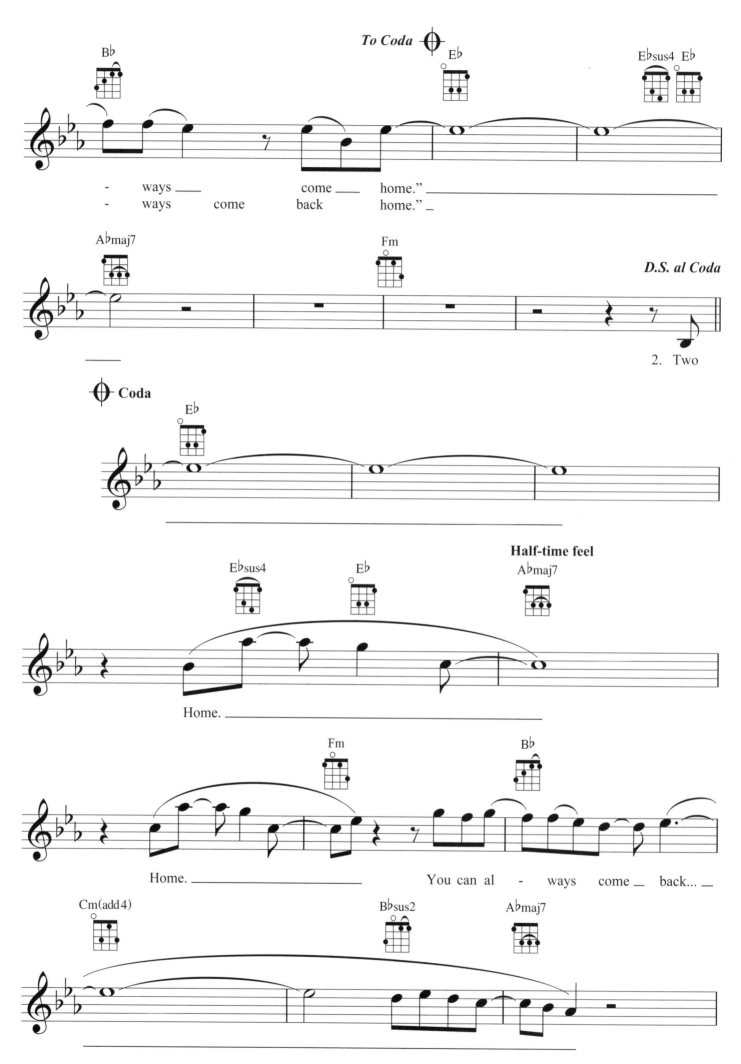

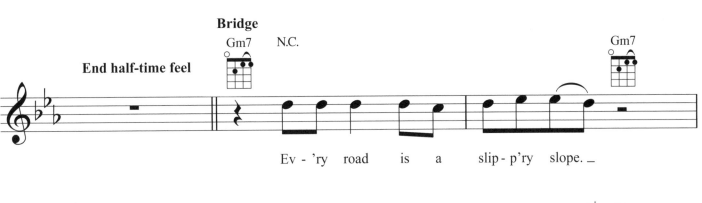

Bridge

Ev - 'ry road is a slip - p'ry slope. __

There is al - ways a hand that you can hold __ on to. __

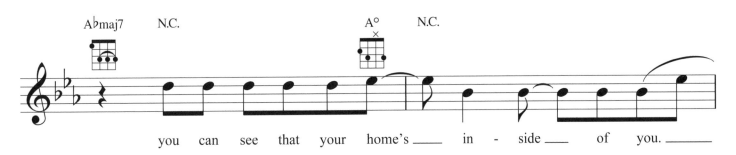

__ Look - ing deep - er through the tel - e - scope, __

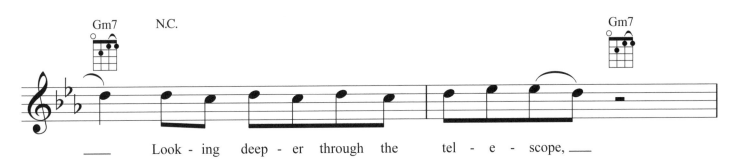

you can see that your home's __ in - side __ of you. __

Chorus

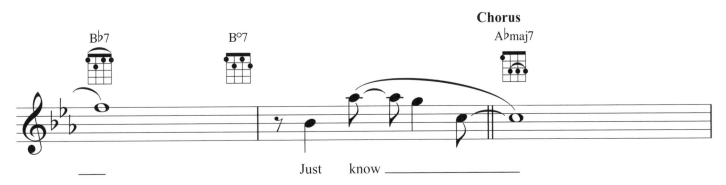

Just know __

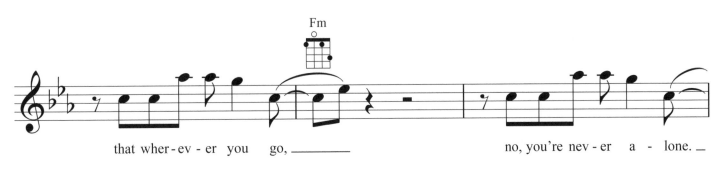

that wher - ev - er you go, __ no, you're nev - er a - lone. __

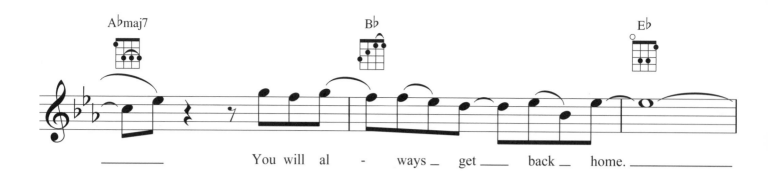

You will al - ways __ get __ back __ home. __

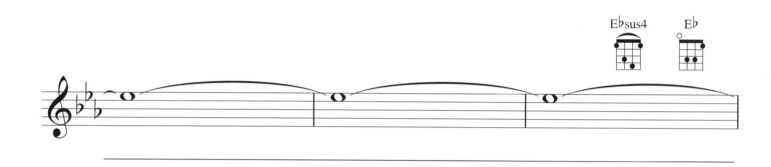

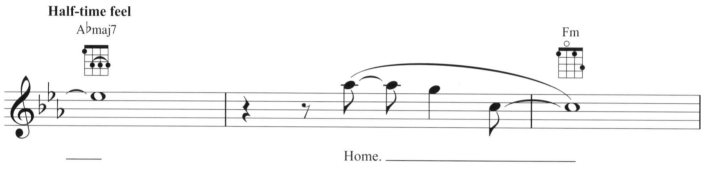

Half-time feel

Home. __

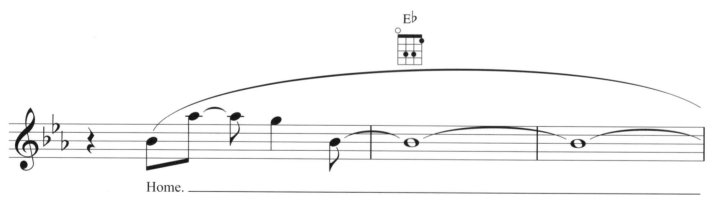

Home. __

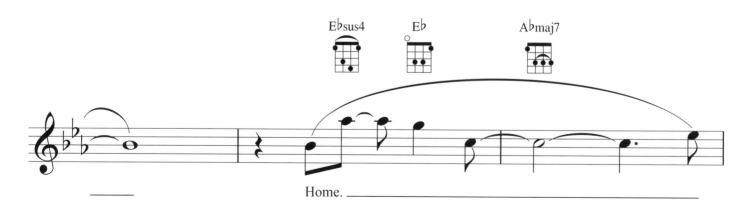

Home. __

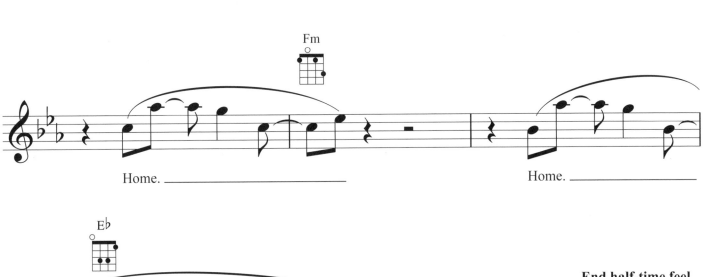

Home. _____

Home. _____

End half-time feel

Outro-Verse

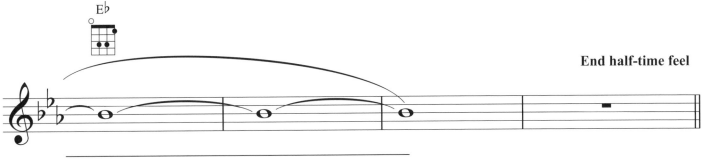

Nine-ty-three mil-lion miles ___ from the sun. Peo-ple, get read-y, get

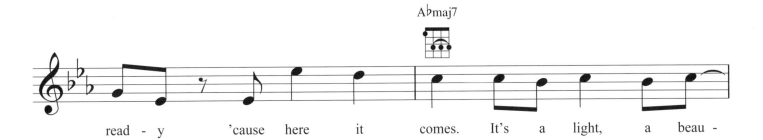

read - y   'cause   here   it   comes.   It's   a   light,   a   beau -

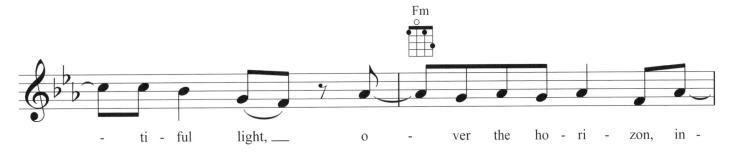

- ti - ful   light, ___   o - ver   the   ho - ri - zon,   in -

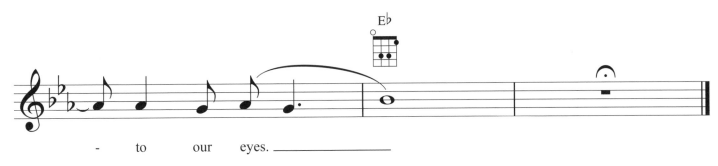

- to   our   eyes. _____

You and I Both

Words and Music by Jason Mraz

First note

Verse
Moderately ♩ = 99

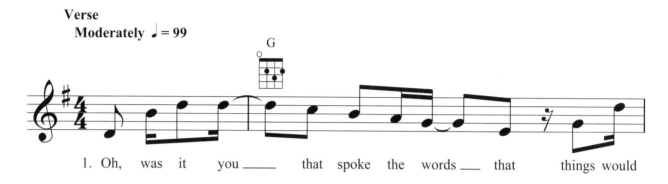

1. Oh, was it you ___ that spoke the words ___ that things would

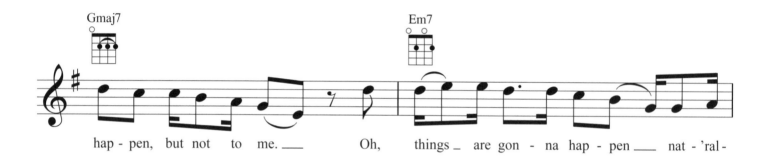

hap - pen, but not to me. ___ Oh, things _ are gon - na hap - pen ___ nat - 'ral -

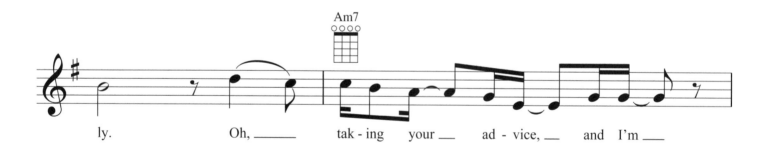

ly. Oh, ___ tak - ing your ___ ad - vice, ___ and I'm ___

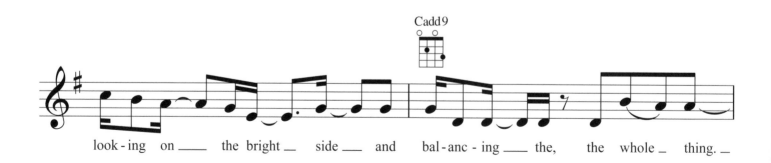

look - ing on ___ the bright ___ side ___ and bal - anc - ing ___ the, the whole _ thing. ___

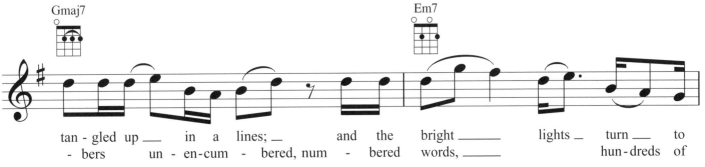

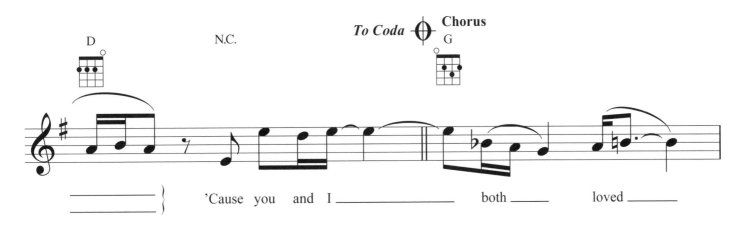

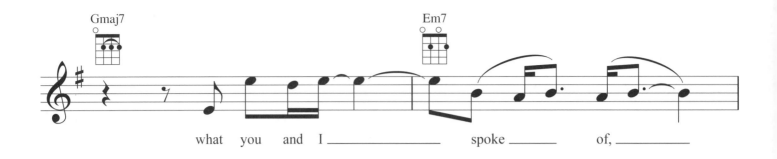

what you and I _____ spoke _____ of, _____

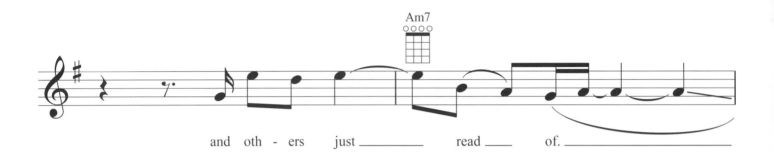

and oth - ers just _____ read ___ of. _____

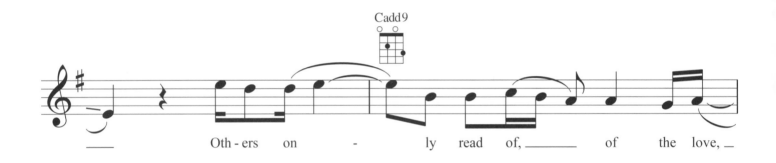

___ Oth - ers on - ly read of, _____ of the love, ___

_____ of the love that I _____ love, _____ yeah. ___

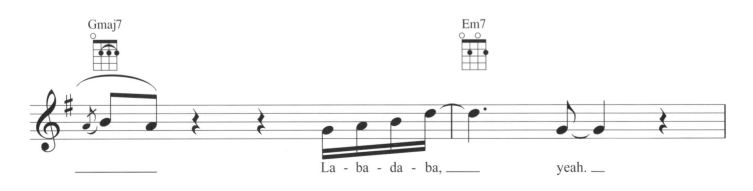

_____ La - ba - da - ba, _____ yeah. ___

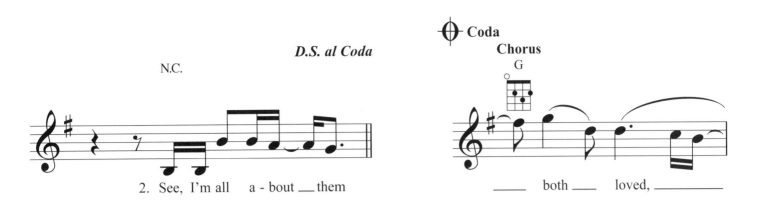

D.S. al Coda

Coda
Chorus

N.C.

2. See, I'm all a - bout them ___ both ___ loved, _____

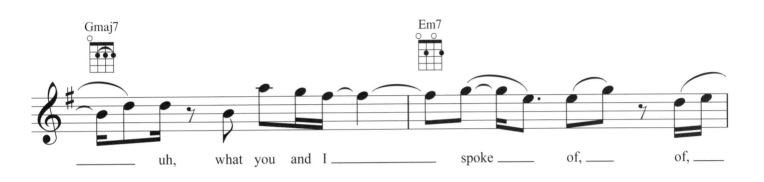

_____ uh, what you and I _____ spoke ___ of, ___ of, ___

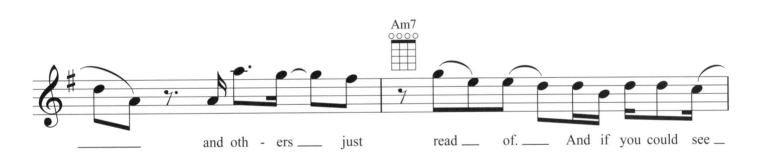

_____ and oth - ers ___ just read ___ of. ___ And if you could see ___

___ me now, ___ oh, love, ___ love. ___ You and I, ___ you and I, ___

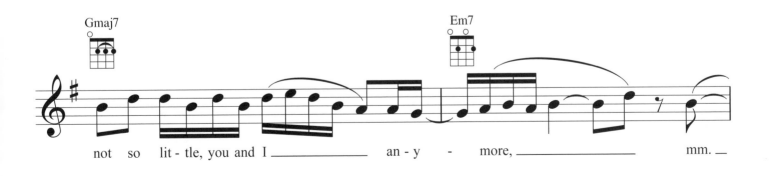

not so lit - tle, you and I _____ an - y - more, _____ mm. ___

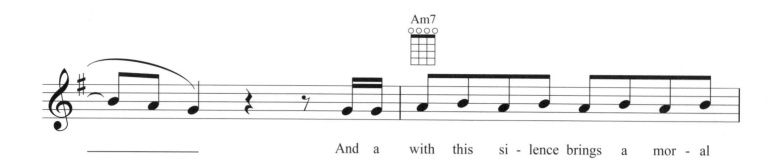

And a with this si - lence brings a mor - al

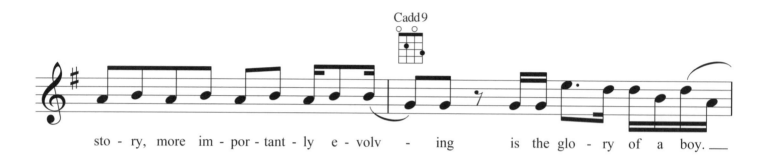

sto - ry, more im - por - tant - ly e - volv - ing is the glo - ry of a boy.

𝄋𝄋 Chorus

'Cause you and I _____ both _____ loved, _____

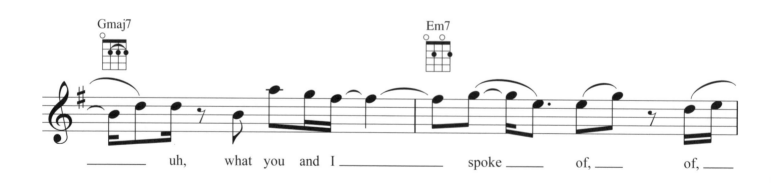

uh, what you and I _____ spoke _____ of, _____ of, _____

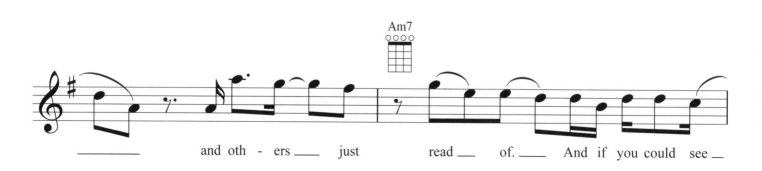

_____ and oth - ers ____ just read __ of. ____ And if you could see _____

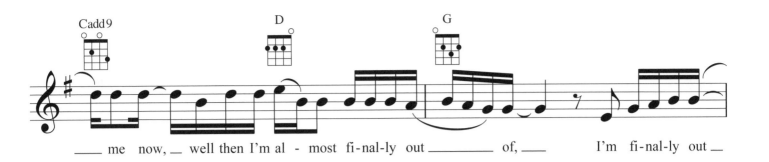

me now, __ well then I'm al - most fi-nal-ly out _____ of, __ I'm fi-nal-ly out __

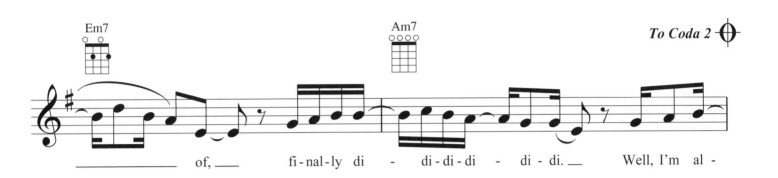

To Coda 2

_____ of, __ fi-nal-ly di - di-di-di - di-di. __ Well, I'm al -

- most fi - nal-ly, fi - nal-ly, well, I _____ am free. Oh, __ I'm

Bridge

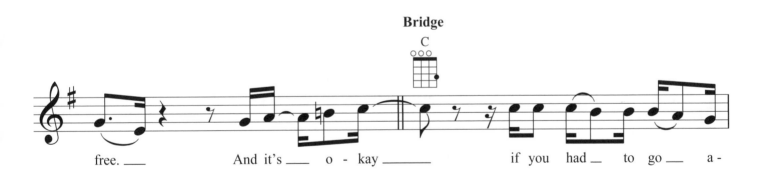

free. __ And it's __ o - kay _____ if you had __ to go __ a -

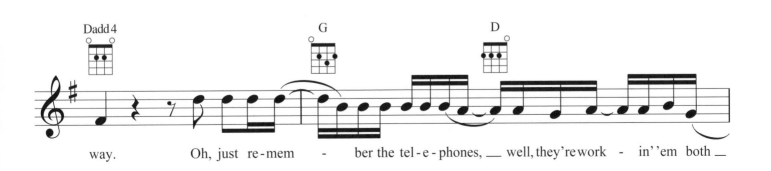

way. Oh, just re-mem - ber the tel-e-phones, __ well, they're work - in' 'em both __

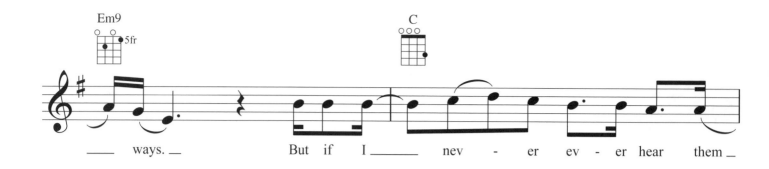

ways. But if I nev - er ev - er hear them

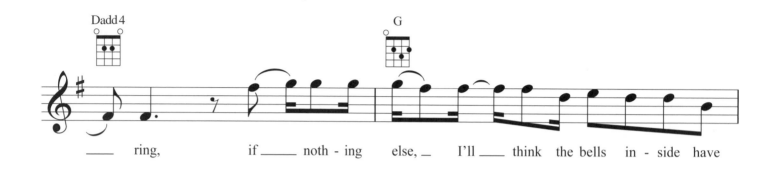

ring, if nothing else, I'll think the bells inside have

fi - n'lly found you some - one else. And that's o - kay,

D.S.S. al Coda 2

'cause I'll re - mem - ber ev - 'ry - thing you say. 'Cause you and I

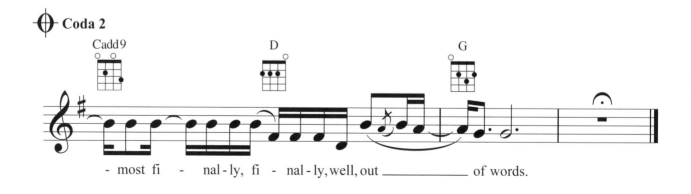

- most fi - nal - ly, fi - nal - ly, well, out of words.

HAL•LEONARD
UKULELE
PLAY-ALONG®

Now you can play your favorite songs on your uke with great-sounding backing tracks to help you sound like a bona fide pro! This series includes the Amazing Slow Downer, so you can adjust the tempo without changing the pitch.

1. POP HITS
00701451 Book/CD Pack....................... $14.99

2. UKE CLASSICS
00701452 Book/CD Pack....................... $12.99

3. HAWAIIAN FAVORITES
00701453 Book/CD Pack....................... $12.99

4. CHILDREN'S SONGS
00701454 Book/CD Pack....................... $12.99

5. CHRISTMAS SONGS
00701696 Book/CD Pack....................... $12.99

6. LENNON & McCARTNEY
00701723 Book/CD Pack....................... $12.99

7. DISNEY FAVORITES
00701724 Book/CD Pack....................... $12.99

8. CHART HITS
00701745 Book/CD Pack....................... $14.99

9. THE SOUND OF MUSIC
00701784 Book/CD Pack....................... $12.99

10. MOTOWN
00701964 Book/CD Pack....................... $12.99

11. CHRISTMAS STRUMMING
00702458 Book/CD Pack....................... $12.99

12. BLUEGRASS FAVORITES
00702584 Book/CD Pack....................... $12.99

13. UKULELE SONGS
00702599 Book/CD Pack....................... $12.99

14. JOHNNY CASH
00702615 Book/CD Pack....................... $14.99

15. COUNTRY CLASSICS
00702834 Book/CD Pack....................... $12.99

16. STANDARDS
00702835 Book/CD Pack....................... $12.99

17. POP STANDARDS
00702836 Book/CD Pack....................... $12.99

18. IRISH SONGS
00703086 Book/CD Pack....................... $12.99

19. BLUES STANDARDS
00703087 Book/CD Pack....................... $12.99

20. FOLK POP ROCK
00703088 Book/CD Pack....................... $12.99

21. HAWAIIAN CLASSICS
00703097 Book/CD Pack....................... $12.99

22. ISLAND SONGS
00703098 Book/CD Pack....................... $12.99

23. TAYLOR SWIFT
00704106 Book/CD Pack....................... $14.99

24. WINTER WONDERLAND
00101871 Book/CD Pack....................... $12.99

25. GREEN DAY
00110398 Book/CD Pack....................... $14.99

26. BOB MARLEY
00110399 Book/CD Pack....................... $14.99

27. TIN PAN ALLEY
00116358 Book/CD Pack....................... $12.99

28. STEVIE WONDER
00116736 Book/CD Pack....................... $14.99

30. ACOUSTIC SONGS
00122336 Book/CD Pack....................... $14.99

32. TOP DOWNLOADS
00127507 Book/CD Pack....................... $14.99

34. CHRISTMAS HITS
00128602 Book/CD Pack....................... $14.99

HAL•LEONARD® CORPORATION

7777 W. BLUEMOUND RD. P.O. BOX 13819 MILWAUKEE, WI 53213

www.halleonard.com

Prices, contents, and availability subject to change without notice.

0814

Ride the Ukulele Wave!

The Beach Boys for Ukulele

This folio features 20 favorites, including: Barbara Ann • Be True to Your School • California Girls • Fun, Fun, Fun • God Only Knows • Good Vibrations • Help Me Rhonda • I Get Around • In My Room • Kokomo • Little Deuce Coupe • Sloop John B • Surfin' U.S.A. • Wouldn't It Be Nice • and more!

00701726 . . . . $14.99

Disney Songs for Ukulele

20 great Disney classics arranged for all uke players, including: Beauty and the Beast • Bibbidi-Bobbidi-Boo (The Magic Song) • Can You Feel the Love Tonight • Chim Chim Cher-ee • Heigh-Ho • It's a Small World • Some Day My Prince Will Come • We're All in This Together • When You Wish upon a Star • and more.

00701708 . . . . $12.99

Jack Johnson – Strum & Sing

Cherry Lane Music
Strum along with 41 Jack Johnson songs using this top-notch collection of chords and lyrics just for the uke! Includes: Better Together • Bubble Toes • Cocoon • Do You Remember • Flake • Fortunate Fool • Good People • Holes to Heaven • Taylor • Tomorrow Morning • and more.

02501702 . . . . $14.99

The Beatles for Ukulele

Ukulele players can strum, sing and pick along with 20 Beatles classics! Includes: All You Need Is Love • Eight Days a Week • Good Day Sunshine • Here, There and Everywhere • Let It Be • Love Me Do • Penny Lane • Yesterday • and more.

00700154 . . . . $16.99

Folk Songs for Ukulele

A great collection to take along to the campfire! 60 folk songs, including: Amazing Grace • Buffalo Gals • Camptown Races • For He's a Jolly Good Fellow • Good Night Ladies • Home on the Range • I've Been Working on the Railroad • Kumbaya • My Bonnie Lies over the Ocean • On Top of Old Smoky • Scarborough Fair • Swing Low, Sweet Chariot • Take Me Out to the Ball Game • Yankee Doodle • and more.

00696068 . . . . $12.99

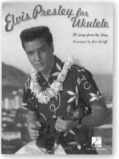

Elvis Presley for Ukulele

arr. Jim Beloff
20 classic hits from The King: All Shook Up • Blue Hawaii • Blue Suede Shoes • Can't Help Falling in Love • Don't • Heartbreak Hotel • Hound Dog • Jailhouse Rock • Love Me • Love Me Tender • Return to Sender • Suspicious Minds • Teddy Bear • and more.

00701004 . . . . $14.99

The Daily Ukulele

compiled and arranged by
Liz and Jim Beloff
Strum a different song everyday with easy arrangements of 365 of your favorite songs in one big songbook! Includes favorites by the Beatles, Beach Boys, and Bob Dylan, folk songs, pop songs, kids' songs, Christmas carols, and Broadway and Hollywood tunes, all with a spiral binding for ease of use.

00240356 . . . . $34.99

Glee

Music from the Fox Television Show for Ukulele
20 favorites for Gleeks to strum and sing, including: Bad Romance • Beautiful • Defying Gravity • Don't Stop Believin' • No Air • Proud Mary • Rehab • True Colors • and more.

00701722 . . . . $14.99

Jake Shimabukuro – Peace Love Ukulele

Deemed "the Hendrix of the ukulele," Hawaii native Jake Shimabukuro is a uke virtuoso. Our songbook features note-for-note transcriptions with ukulele tablature of Jake's masterful playing on all the CD tracks: Bohemian Rhapsody • Boy Meets Girl • Bring Your Adz • Hallelujah • Pianoforte 2010 • Variation on a Dance 2010 • and more, plus two bonus selections!

00702516 . . . . $19.99

The Daily Ukulele – Leap Year Edition

366 More Songs for Better Living
compiled and arranged by
Liz and Jim Beloff
An amazing second volume with 366 MORE songs for you to master each day of a leap year! Includes: Ain't No Sunshine • Calendar Girl • I Got You Babe • Lean on Me • Moondance • and many, many more.

00240681 . . . . $34.99

Hawaiian Songs for Ukulele

Over thirty songs from the state that made the ukulele famous, including: Beyond the Rainbow • Hanalei Moon • Ka-lu-a • Lovely Hula Girl • Mele Kalikimaka • One More Aloha • Sea Breeze • Tiny Bubbles • Waikiki • and more.

00696065 . . . . $9.99

Worship Songs for Ukulele

25 worship songs: Amazing Grace (My Chains are Gone) • Blessed Be Your Name • Enough • God of Wonders • Holy Is the Lord • How Great Is Our God • In Christ Alone • Love the Lord • Mighty to Save • Sing to the King • Step by Step • We Fall Down • and more.

00702546 . . . . $12.99

HAL•LEONARD® CORPORATION
7777 W. Bluemound Rd. P.O. Box 13819 Milwaukee, WI 53213

Disney characters and artwork © Disney Enterprises, Inc.

Prices, contents, and availability subject to change.

1114